AMERICAN RECIPES

Favorite and Traditional Recipes of African American Cooking

(Easy and Delicious American Classic Recipes)

Willie Cribb

Published by Sharon Lohan

© Willie Cribb

All Rights Reserved

American Recipes: Favorite and Traditional Recipes of African American Cooking (Easy and Delicious American Classic Recipes)

ISBN 978-1-7776245-1-4

All rights reserved. No part of this guide may be reproduced in any form without permission in writing from the publisher except in the case of brief quotations embodied in critical articles or reviews.

Legal & Disclaimer

The information contained in this book is not designed to replace or take the place of any form of medicine or professional medical advice. The information in this book has been provided for educational and entertainment purposes only.

The information contained in this book has been compiled from sources deemed reliable, and it is accurate to the best of the Author's knowledge; however, the Author cannot guarantee its accuracy and validity and cannot be held liable for any errors or omissions. Changes are periodically made to this book. You must consult your doctor or get professional medical advice before using any of the suggested remedies, techniques, or information in this book.

Table of contents

Part 1 1

Introduction 2

Illinois - Classic Chicago Hot Dog 4

Indiana - Tenderloin Sandwiches With Creamy Corn Relish 6

Iowa - Corn Casserole 9

Kansas - Meatloaf With Brown Sugar And Ketchup Glaze 11

Kentucky - Bourbon Burgoo 13

Louisiana - Mock Turtle Soup 16

Maine - Codfish Balls 19

Maryland - Chesapeake Chowder 21

Massachusetts - Boston Baked Beans 23

Michigan - Traditional Cornish Pasties 25

Minnesota - Swedish Meatballs 28

Mississippi - Catfish And Hushpuppies 30

Missouri - Barbecue Ribs 33

Montana - Wild Huckleberry Pie 35

Nebraska - Kolache 37

Nevada - Frank's Clams Posillipo 39

New Hampshire - Seafood Chowder With Lobster 42

New Jersey - Chinese Beef With Jersey Tomatoes 46

New Mexico - Green Chili Apple Pie 48

New York – Classic Baked Vanilla Cheesecake 51

North Carolina - Sweet Potato Pie 54

North Dakota - Knoephla Soup 56

Ohio - Buckeyes 58

Oklahoma - Chicken-Fried Steak And Gravy 60

Oregon - Marionberry Cream Cheese Pie 62

Pennsylvania - Root Beer Beef Stew 65

Rhode Island - Baked Apples And Sausage 68

South Carolina - Old Charleston Style Shrimp And Grits 70

South Dakota – Kuchen 73

Tennessee - Elvis Presley's Baked Ham In Cola 76

Texas - Beef Chili Con Carne 78

Utah - Sweet Onion Soup 80

Vermont - Maple Syrup Pork Chops 82

Virginia - Cream Of Peanut Soup 85

Washington - Chili Half-Smokes 87

West Virginia - Barbecued Bear 90

Wisconsin - Beer Brats 92

Wyoming - Tenderloin Of Beef 94

Part 2 96

Introduction 97

Chapter 1: Healthy And Nutritious American Desserts Recipes 99

Recipe #1: The Malt Hot Chocolate S'mores 100

Recipe #2: Brown Rice With Date And Carrot Puddings 102

#3: Recipe #76: Apple Coffeecake 104

Recipe #4: The Brownie Strawberry Trifle 106

Chapter 2: The Very Delicious American Meaty Collections 107

Recipe #5: The Smokey Pot With Boston Beans 108

Recipe #6: The Griddled Chicken Served With Corn Cobs And Gem Lettuce Salad. 110

Recipe #7: The Crispy Cashew Chicken 112

#8: Beef With The Lentil Burger 114

Chapter 3: Scrumptious And Filling Snacks Recipes 116

Recipe #9: The Choc-Chip Pecan Pie 117

Recipe #10: The Bourbon With Black Cherry And Bacon Brownies 120

Recipe #11: Fresh Fruit With Yoghurt Ice Pops 122

Recipe #12: Simple And Fast Vanilla Cupcakes 123

Chapter 4: Amazing Seafood And Poultry Recipes 125

Recipe #13: Baked Fish Served With Vegetables 126

Recipe #14: Ginger Sesame Salmon 128

Recipe #15: The Hearty Fish Stew 129

Recipe #16: The Lemon Salmon Served With Kaffir Lime... 131

Chapter 5: Low-Calorie Bread And Related Recipes............ 133

Recipe #17: The Keto Banana Loaf 134

Recipe #18: The Gluten-Free Coconut And Almond Bread. 135

Recipe #19: The American Cornbread 137

Chapter 6: Amazing Soups And Stews Worth Relishing 139

Recipe #20: The Tomato Soup 140

Recipe #21: The Minestrone Soup.. 142

Recipe #22: The Poblano Black Bean Corn Soup...................... 144

Recipe #23: The Quick And Easy Vegetable Curry 145

Conclusion.. 147

Part 1

Introduction

Peach Cobbler baking in the oven, Mississippi Mud Pie chilling in the refrigerator and Baby Back Ribs cooking on the grill. These are all recipes that readily spring to mind when we consider the culinary delights of the USA.

American cuisine, however, is far more fascinating and diverse.

The USA is a melting pot of cultures and thanks to its many hundreds and thousands of immigrants, offers a combination of tastes and flavors from around the world.

Over the centuries, settlers and immigrants were bringing with them new herbs and spices, not to mention recipes from their homelands including Kuchen (cake) and Knoephla (potato dumpling soup).

Lots of foods considered to be American have their roots planted firmly in other countries around the world. Take for example pizza; deep dish in Chicago, thin crust in New York but created in Naples, Italy.

You could say that all American food depends almost entirely on where you are in the country.

Peaches abound in Georgia; oranges are plentiful in Florida, while tomatoes thrive in New Jersey.

Beef is in abundant supply in Texas and Wyoming, and seafood is readily available in Louisiana and New England.

Illinois - Classic Chicago Hot Dog

This favorite street food appears to have somewhat of a sad history, being sold originally during the Great Depression of 1929.

Desperate Chicagoans bought this special sandwich for just one nickel, and so the 'dog' became known as the Depression Sandwich.

From humble beginnings, the 'dog in a bun' has gone on to have its very own National Hot Dog Day in July of each year.

Portions: 8

Prep Time: **5mins**

Total Time: **15mins**

Ingredients:
- Cold water
- 8 Vienna 100% beef hot dogs
- 2 pounds Idaho potatoes (unpeeled, cut into 3" long an ½" thick fries)
- Sea salt and black pepper (to season)

- 8 poppy seed hot dog/burger buns
- I cup fresh tomatoes (seeded)
- 1 cup onion (minced)
- 1 cup yellow mustard
- 1 cup sweet relish
- Sport peppers (to taste)
- Celery salt (to taste)

Directions:

1. Preheat a fryer.

2. Fill a large pot or pan, 75% full with cold water, and swiftly bring to boil.

3. Add the 8 hot dogs and reduce the temperature to a simmer. Cover the pot.

4. Cook the dogs for 6-8 minutes; or until they plump.

5. Fry the chipped potatoes for 5-7 minutes, stirring, until lightly brown all over. Remove the potatoes from the pan and drain off any excess fat using kitchen paper towel. Season well with sea salt and black pepper.

6. Lay the dogs inside the buns, topping each one with 2-3 tablespoons each of, tomatoes, onions, yellow mustard and sweet pickle relish. Topping with peppers and seasoning with a dash of celery salt.

7. Place each of the hot dogs in the middle of a sheet of deli wrapping. Place the French fries alongside the hot dog and wrap tightly.

Indiana - Tenderloin Sandwiches With Creamy Corn Relish

This pork sandwich is similar to a Wiener schnitzel and is hugely popular in Indiana. The main difference being that the pork loin is deep fried rather than pan fried like the Schnitzel, which was brought to the US in the 19th century by German immigrants.

Portions: 4

Prep Time: **35mins**

Total Time: **35mins**

Ingredients:

- 2 tsp butter
- ½ cup fresh corn kernels
- ⅛ tsp ground red pepper
- 1 tbsp. 2% reduced-fat milk
- 1 tbsp. cider vinegar
- 2 ounces low-fat cream cheese (softened)
- 3 tbsp. red bell pepper (diced)
- 1 tbsp. diced red onion (diced)

- 1 tbsp. fresh parsley (chopped)
- 4 (3-ounce) slices pork tenderloin
- ½ tsp salt
- ½ tsp freshly ground black pepper
- 1 large egg
- 1 tsp water
- 2 tbsp. quick-mixing flour
- ⅔ cup panko (Japanese breadcrumbs)
- Peanut oil (for deep frying)
- 4 green leaf lettuce leaves
- 4 white-wheat hamburger buns

Directions:

1. In a small frying pan or skillet, over moderate to high heat, melt the butter.

2. Add the corn along with the red pepper and sauté for 2-3 minutes, or until tender yet crisp.

3. Add the reduced-fat milk, cider vinegar, and cream cheese and cook for 60 seconds or until the cream cheese begins to melt, while continually stirring.

4. Remove the frying pan from the heat and stir in the bell pepper together with the onion and parsley. Allow the pan to stand at room temperature.

5. Lay the slices of pork between 2 pieces of plastic wrap and using a heavy object such as a rolling pin pound the pork to an even thickness of 1/4". Discard the wrap.

6. Evenly sprinkle the pork with salt and pepper.

7. In a shallow bowl, combine the egg with 1 teaspoon of cold water, and using a hand whisk, stir.

8. Place the flour and panko in separate bowls.

9. Dredge the pork slices in the flour, dip the pork in the egg and dredge in the panko.

10. Over moderate to high heat, in a large frying or skillet, heat ¼-½" the peanut oil.

11. Add the pork and cook for 3-4 minutes on each side, until a deep-fry thermometer registers 360 degrees F, or until sufficiently cooked through and golden brown.

12. Remove from pan and drain on kitchen paper towels.

13. Lay 1 lettuce leaf on the bottom half of each of the buns and top with a slice of pork.

14. Dollop 2-3 tablespoons of corn relish on top of the pork and top with the other half of the bun.

Iowa - Corn Casserole

Iowa harvests so much corn that it's earned the nickname, the Corn State. In fact, the land where 'the tall corn grows' leads the USA in corn production.

Portions: 6-8

Prep Time: **15mins**

Total Time: **35mins**

Ingredients:

- 1 pound bacon (diced)
- 2 cups breadcrumbs
- ¼ cup onion (minced)
- ½ cup green pepper (chopped)
- 2 cans (16.5 ounces) cream style corn

Directions:

1. In a frying pan or skillet, fry the bacon until browned. Remove from the pan and set to one side.

2. Pour between ⅛–¼ cup of pan drippings over the breadcrumbs and put to one side.

3. Discard all except 2 tablespoons of remaining bacon drippings, and sauté the onion and pepper until just tender.

4. Stir in the cream style corn and cooked bacon.

5. Spoon the mixture into a 1-quart casserole dish, sprinkle with breadcrumbs and bake in the oven at 350 degrees F for 20-25 minutes, or until it begins to bubble.

Kansas - Meatloaf With Brown Sugar And Ketchup Glaze

Welcome to cattle country! Kansas, where BBQs are the order of the day and meat figures firmly on the menu. Fried chicken, smoked ribs, steak and meatloaf, all served up with a big old portion of black-eyed peas, corn, green beans or okra.

Portions: 8

Prep Time: **20mins**

Total Time: 1hour 20mins

Ingredients:
- ½ cup ketchup
- ½ cup packed brown sugar
- 1½ tsp salt
- ½ tsp chili powder
- 1½ pounds lean ground beef
- 1½ cups croutons (crushed)

- 1 small onion (chopped)
- 2 medium eggs
- ¼ cup whole milk
- ¼ tsp ground black pepper

Directions:

1. Preheat the main oven to 350 degrees F. Lightly grease a 9x5" loaf pan.

2. First, make the glaze by adding the ketchup, brown sugar, salt, and chili powder to a bowl and stirring until combined and smooth. Spread a small amount of the mixture into the bottom of the loaf pan.

3. To make the meatloaf, in a large mixing bowl combine the ground beef along with the croutons, onion, eggs, milk and black pepper. Shape the mixture into a loaf and place in the prepared pan. Evenly spread any remaining ketchup over the entire loaf.

4. Transfer to the preheated oven and bake until no pink remains; about 60 minutes.

5. A thermometer inserted into the middle of the meatloaf should register a minimum temperature of 160 degrees F.

Kentucky - Bourbon Burgoo

Burgoo is to Kentucky what gumbo is to Louisiana. Lots of people claim the dish belongs to their region and the French say that burgoo is a variation of ragout. One thing everyone agrees upon though is that this meat fest stew should be cooked over an open fire.

Portions: 12-14

Prep Time: **15mins**

Total Time: 12hours 15mins

Ingredients:

- 2 pounds veal shank
- 2 pounds pork shank
- 2 pounds beef shank
- 2 pounds breast of lamb
- 1 (4 pound) chicken
- 8 quarts cold water
- 1½ pounds potato
- 1½ pounds onion
- 1 bunch carrots (scrubbed, peeled, thickly sliced)

- 2 green peppers (seeded, chopped)
- 2 cups cabbage (chopped)
- 1-quart tomato puree
- 2 cups fresh whole corn
- 2 pods red pepper
- 2 cups okra (diced)
- ½ cup parsley (chopped)
- 2 cups dry lima beans
- 1 cup celery (diced)
- ¾ cup Kentucky bourbon
- Salt and pepper
- Tabasco
- Steak Sauce
- Worcestershire sauce

Directions:

1. In a huge pot add the meats (veal through chicken).

2. Add cold water and slowly bring to boil. Simmer for 4-6 hours, until the meat is tender and easily falls off the bones.

3. Remove the meat from the stock and allow to cool before removing it from the bones and chopping. Return the chopped meat to the stock in the pot.

4. Pare the potatoes along with onions and dice. Add them to the pot, along with the carrots, green pepper, chopped cabbage, puree, corn, red pepper, okra, parsley, lima beans, diced celery, and bourbon, to the meat and the stock.

5. Allow the burgoo to simmer for 5-6 hours until thick.

6. Taste and season the burgoo with salt, pepper, Tabasco, steak sauce and Worcestershire sauce.

Louisiana - Mock Turtle Soup

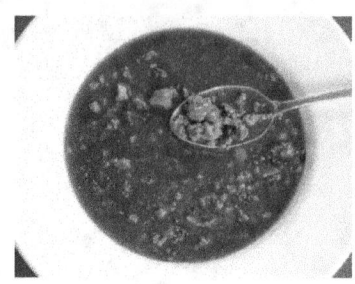

Turtle soup dates back some 300 plus years when the first French settlers caught and ate anything and everything that crossed their path including fish, seafood, gators, and turtle. New Orleans turtle soup is as unique to American cuisine as gumbo and jambalaya and is still served in some restaurants in the French Quarter.

This recipe swaps turtle for ground sirloin, but it tastes just like the real deal.

Portions: 4

Prep Time: **25mins**

Total Time: 5hours 20mins

Ingredients:

- ¾ cup unsalted butter
- 6 celery stalks (chopped)
- 1 cup onion (chopped)
- 2 garlic cloves (minced)

- 1½ pounds ground sirloin
- 1 (15 ounce) can tomato purée
- 1 (14.5 ounce) can chicken broth
- 1 (14.5 ounce) can beef broth
- ½ cup all-purpose flour mixed with 1 cup cold water
- ½ cup Worcestershire sauce
- 1 cup ketchup
- 1 tsp hot sauce
- 2 bay leaves
- 1½ tsp dried thyme
- 1 tsp salt
- ½ tsp ground black pepper
- ½ cup fresh lemon juice
- ¼ cup minced fresh parsley
- 6 large hard-cooked eggs (peeled, chopped)
- ½ cup sherry
- Lemon slices (to garnish)

Directions:

1. In a large pan over moderate to high heat, melt the butter.

2. When melted, add the celery along with the onion, and garlic and cook until just soft, this will take around 5-7 minutes. Add the ground sirloin and cook until the meat is beginning to brown and veggies are tender, this will take around 15 minutes.

3. Transfer the mixture to a slow cooker (8 quarts) and add the puree, broths, flour mixture, Worcestershire sauce, ketchup, hot sauce, bay leaves, thyme, salt, and

pepper, stirring well to combine. Cook over a low heat for 4 hours.

4. Add the lemon juice and continue cooking for 30 minutes.

5. Remove the bay leaves, and stir in the parsley, eggs, and sherry.

6. Garnish with slices of lemon and serve.

Maine - Codfish Balls

New England has the well-deserved reputation for serving up some of the best breakfasts in the country. Diners throughout the state serve up history on a plate, thanks to the many settlers who traveled across the Atlantic to make American their home.

Fish cakes, or breaded and pan-fried balls made with locally caught white fish, were a typical breakfast dish.

Portions: 4-6

Prep Time: **10mins**

Total Time: **37mins**

Ingredients:

- 1½ pounds fresh codfish
- 3 cups raw sweet potatoes (peeled, diced)
- 2 tsp salt
- ½ tsp ground pepper
- 2 tbsp. fresh dill (snipped)
- Cornmeal
- Oil (to deep fry)

Directions:

1. To a large pot or pan, add the cod, sweet potatoes, salt, and pepper, and fill with sufficient water to cover.

2. Cover the pot and over moderate heat, cook for 25 minutes.

3. Remove the pot from the heat and drain.

4. Add the dill and either puree or mash the mixture.

5. Shape the mixture into 3" balls and roll them in the cornmeal, making sure they are evenly coated.

6. In a deep sided pan, heat the oil to 375 degrees F and fry the fish balls for 60 seconds, or until golden.

7. Remove them from the oil, drain, using kitchen paper towels to absorb any excess oil.

8. Serve.

Maryland - Chesapeake Chowder

No Maryland chowder would be complete without a little Old Bay seasoning. Although it's generally added to seafood and crab, locals will sprinkle it on just about anything.

The seasoning was created by Gustav Brunn in 1939. We wonder if Brunn, a German Jewish immigrant, could ever have imagined that nearly 80 years later it would take its place alongside salt and pepper in so many homes.

Portions: 8 cups

Prep Time: **25mins**

Total Time: 1hour 10mins

Ingredients:
- 1 tbsp. olive oil
- 1 onion (chopped)
- 3 garlic cloves (minced)
- 2 celery ribs (chopped)
- ¼ cup all-purpose flour

- 2½ cups chicken broth
- 1 cup dry white wine
- 1 (8 ounce) bottle clam juice
- 5 red potatoes (peeled, diced)
- 1 tbsp. Old Bay seasoning
- ½ pound unpeeled, medium-size fresh shrimp (peeled, deveined)
- ½ pound fresh crabmeat (drained, flaked, shell removed)
- ½ cup heavy cream
- Fresh parsley (chopped)

Directions:

1. In a Dutch oven over moderate to high heat, heat the oil.

2. When the oil is hot, sauté the onion, garlic, and celery for 7-8 minutes, or until just tender.

3. Stir in the flour and while continually stirring, continue cooking for 60 seconds.

4. Add the broth along with the following 4 ingredients and bring to boil. Cover with a lid and reduce the heat, while occasionally stirring for 25-30 minutes, or until the potatoes are just tender.

5. Add the shrimp, crabmeat, and heavy cream and over low heat, cook for 5-6 minutes, or until the shrimp become pink.

6. Garnish with chopped parsley.

Massachusetts - Boston Baked Beans

Baked beans are as American as apple pie and dating back to Colonial times; they are synonymous with the state of Boston.

When you can add a little rum, sweet molasses, and bacon, why would you ever want store-bought baked beans?

Portions: 10-12

Prep Time: **25mins**

Total Time: 14hours 45mins

Ingredients:
- 4 cups (2 pounds) pea beans
- 2 whole cloves
- 1 medium-large onion
- 1 tsp baking soda
- 1 pound bacon (rind removed, cut into ¼" cubes)
- 1½ cups dark molasses (not blackstrap)
- 2 tsp mustard (ground)
- 2 tbsp. kosher salt

- Freshly ground black pepper
- 2 tbsp. dark rum

Directions:

1. In a mixing bowl add the beans along with sufficient cold water to cover by 3" and allow them to soak overnight.

2. Heat the main oven to 275 degrees F and position the oven rack in the lower third of the oven.

3. Drain the soaked beans and transfer to a 6 quart, heavy pot or Dutch oven. Add enough cold water to cover the beans by 1".

4. Gently but firmly press the cloves into the onion and place the onion along with the baking soda in the pot and stir well to combine.

5. On the top of the stove, over high heat, bring the beans to boil.

6. Reduce the heat to low, skimming off any surface foam, and simmer for 15 minutes. Add the remaining ingredients and stir well until incorporated.

7. Place the pot in the oven and bake for 5-6 hours, or until the beans are just tender, adding a drop of water if needed.

8. Allow the surface of the beans to slightly crust over during the final half hour of baking.

9. Serve.

Michigan - Traditional Cornish Pasties

Michiganian can thank the Cornish immigrants of the 19th century for introducing them to pasties.

History reveals that Cornish underground tin miners, unable to return to the surface to eat, would enjoy a hearty lunchtime pasty. The thick crust kept their dirty working hands from spoiling the meat inside.

Portions: 4

Prep Time: **15mins**

Total Time: 1hour 45mins

Ingredients:

Pastry:

- 1 cup all-purpose flour
- 2 ounces salted butter (cubed)
- Pinch of sea salt
- 2-3 tbsp. cold water

Filling:

- ¼ cup onions (finely chopped)

- ½ cup each swede and potato (chopped)
- ½ cup rump steak (cubes)
- Sea salt and black pepper
- 1 medium egg (beaten lightly)

Directions:

1. Pre-heat the main oven to 425 degrees F.

2. In a large mixing bowl, combine the all-purpose flour with the cubed butter and sea salt.

3. Using clean fingertips rub the butter into the flour until the mixture forms a breadcrumb consistency, work as quickly as possible to prevent the dough becoming too warm.

4. Add 2 tablespoons of cold water to the mixture stirring with a chilled utensil until the dough binds nicely.

5. Wrap the dough in plastic wrap and refrigerate for between 15-30 minutes.

6. Evenly divide the pastry dough in 4 pieces and roll into 6-7" rounds.

7. Put the onion, swede, potato and cubes of rump steak into a bowl and combine. Season the mixture generously with salt and pepper.

8. Divide the mixture between each pastry round and set aside. Brush the edges of the rounds with beaten egg.

9. Fold each round in half, to cover the filling, so that the two edges meet. Using a fork, crimp the edges

together to make a tight seal. Use any remaining egg to brush the pasties all over.

10. Transfer the pasties to a lightly greased baking tray and bake in the preheated oven until golden.

11. Ideally, serve hot.

Minnesota - Swedish Meatballs

For more than 150 years, Swedish immigrants have left their stamp on Minnesota's food culture.

Swedish meatballs are one such dish, and in this version, we add coffee to the sauce for a more rich and complex flavor.

Portions: 8

Prep Time: **10mins**

Total Time: **36mins**

Ingredients:

- 1½ cups bread crumbs
- ⅔ cup half & half
- 1 medium egg (lightly beaten)
- ½ large onion (finely chopped)
- ¼ cup fresh parsley (finely snipped)
- ½ tsp kosher salt
- ⅛ tsp ground ginger
- ⅛ tsp ground nutmeg

- ¾ pound ground beef
- ½ pound ground veal
- ¼ pound ground pork
- 2 tbsp. butter
- 2 tbsp. all-purpose flour
- ⅔ cup half & half
- 1¼ cups water
- 1 tsp instant beef bouillon granules
- ½ tsp instant coffee crystals

Directions:

1. In a large bowl, combine the bread crumbs and 2/3 cup of half & half. Allow to soak for 5-6 minutes.

2. Add the lightly beaten egg along with the onion, fresh parsley, kosher salt, ground ginger, and nutmeg. Add the beef, veal, and pork to the mixture and stir well to combine. Mold the mixture into 1¼" balls.

3. Arrange the meatballs in a baking dish and heat an oven at 350 degrees F for between 15-20 minutes. When cooked through and no pink meat remains, absorb any excess fat by laying the meatballs on kitchen paper towels.

4. In the meantime, melt the butter in a large frying pan. Stir in the remaining half & half, along with the water, instant beef granules, and coffee.

5. Cook, while stirring, until the mixture bubbles and thickens. Add the meatballs to the pan, for 60 seconds, or until heated through.

6. Serve.

Mississippi - Catfish And Hushpuppies

Plantation slaves regularly ate catfish, and due to its local availability, it quickly became a cheap source of protein for even the poorest of people.

But that was 170 years ago, and today, this humble fish proudly symbolizes the state of Mississippi; as a healthy and sustainable food source.

Portions: 4

Prep Time: **10mins**

Total Time: 1hour 25mins

Ingredients:

Hushpuppies:

- 1 cup all-purpose flour
- 2 cups yellow cornmeal
- 1 medium egg
- 1 tbsp. sugar
- 1 tsp salt

- 4 scallions (chopped including stem)
- Buttermilk
- Peanut oil

Catfish:

- 2 cups yellow cornmeal
- ¼ cup all-purpose flour
- 2 tbsp. freshly ground black pepper
- 1 tbsp. lemon pepper
- 1 tsp paprika
- Granulated garlic
- Salt
- 2 cups milk
- ⅛ tsp hot pepper sauce
- 4 catfish fillets (preferably Mississippi pond-raised)
- Peanut oil

Directions:

1. Add the first 6 hushpuppy ingredients to a large mixing bowl.

2. Add the buttermilk as required, until it reaches a consistency similar to mash potatoes.

3. Transfer to the fridge for 45-60 minutes.

4. In an oven, heated to 325 degrees F, heat the peanut oil.

5. Using 2 spoons drop the batter by dipping the 1 spoon into cold water before filling with hushpuppy batter. Use the second spoon to rake the batter into the peanut oil.

6. Cook for 4-5 minutes, until golden.

7. Ideally, the hushpuppies should independently roll around in the oil. If they don't, turn them.

8. For the catfish. Put the first 6 ingredients into a big brown bag. Roll the top of the bag down and shake until they are well mixed.

9. Cut the fish in half lengthwise and pat dry using kitchen paper towel.

10. Combine the milk with the hot sauce.

11. Dip the fish in the milk mixture and when evenly coated put it in the bag and shake it all about until it is covered in the crumb mixture.

12. Transfer the catfish to the pot with around 4" of peanut oil, heat to 350 degrees F.

13. Cook until golden brown and firm, for 6-7 minutes. The fish should flake easily when using a fork.

Missouri - Barbecue Ribs

Missouri is famous for its smoked ribs and steaks.

So, with the greater St Louis area consuming more barbecue sauce per capita than any other USA city, it makes perfect sense for this finger-lickin' good barbecue rib recipe to represent this state.

Portions: 6

Prep Time: **10mins**

Total Time: 4hours 10mins

Ingredients:

- Salt
- Sugar
- 2 tbsp. ground cumin
- Freshly ground black pepper
- 2 tbsp. chili powder
- 4 tbsp. paprika
- 2 (3 pounds each) full racks pork spareribs
- 1¾ cups white vinegar
- 2 tbsp. hot pepper sauce

Directions:

1. In a large mixing bowl combine 2 tablespoons of salt, along with 4 tablespoons of sugar, cumin, 2 tablespoons pepper, chili powder and paprika. Rub the dry mixture over the ribs.

2. Transfer the ribs to baking sheet and bake in the middle of the oven at 325 degrees F for 2½ -3hours.

3. Over a very low charcoal fire and with the rack as high as possible, grill the ribs until a light crust forms on the surface, for up to 25-30 minutes each side. Flip the ribs over and repeat the process.

4. In a mixing bowl combine the vinegar along with the hot pepper sauce, 2 tablespoons sugar, 1 tablespoon salt and 1 tablespoon pepper. Baste the ribs with the mixture and just before removing them from the grill.

Montana - Wild Huckleberry Pie

If Montana had an official food, it would be the huckleberry; a close relation to the blueberry. The state claims itself as being the wild huckleberry capital of the west.

These little berries make the perfect pie, with the blue and purple varieties being sweeter than the bright red.

Watch out though; bears can't get enough of them!

Portions: 1 pie

Prep Time: **15mins**

Total Time: 1hour 10mins

Ingredients:
- Flour (for rolling pastry)
- Fresh pastry for 2 (9") pie crusts
- 5 cups northwest wild blue huckleberries
- 1½ cups sugar
- 5 tbsp. cornstarch
- 4 tbsp. tapioca

- 1 tsp fresh lemon rind (grated)
- 3 tbsp. butter

Directions:

1. Preheat the main oven to 450 degrees F.

2. Flour your rolling pin. Roll the pastry into disc 2" larger than the diameter of your pie dish. Ease the rolled pastry into the pie dish, firmly press into the base and sides. Set to one side.

3. In a mixing bowl, combine all of the ingredients and using a spoon, mix until incorporated.

4. Transfer the mixture into the pastry shell.

5. Dot the surface of the mixture with a few dabs of butter.

6. Trim the pastry leaving only a ½" overhanging.

7. Transfer the pie to the center shelf of the oven and bake for 15 minutes, before turning the heat down to 350 degrees F. Continue baking for 35-40 minutes, or until the filling bubbles over.

8. The pie is cooked once the crust is golden brown.

9. Remove from oven and allow to cool before serving.

Nebraska - Kolache

For those of us not in the culinary know, a kolache is a type of pastry that holds a dollop of fresh fruit and is rimmed by a pillow of puffy dough. They were served initially throughout Central Europe as a wedding dessert.

A large number of Czech immigrants settled in the state of Nebraska, and so kolaches have been popular for a long time.

Portions: 4-6

Prep Time: **15mins**

Total Time: **2hours**

Ingredients:

- 1½ cups whole milk
- 1½ sticks margarine
- 1 tbsp. salt
- ⅔ cup sugar
- 3 tbsp. dry yeast
- ¾ cup warm water

- 3 medium eggs
- ½ cup potato flakes
- 5½ cups flour
- Fruit filling of choice

Directions:

1. In a small pan, scald the milk.

2. Remove the pan from the stove and add the margarine along with the salt and sugar. Stir to combine and until totally melted. Put to one side to cool down.

3. In a bowl, dissolve the yeast in the warm water.

4. Beat the eggs; add the potato flakes, along with the cool milk mixture and yeast.

5. Sift the flour into the mixture and knead well with your hands.

6. Grease bowl and place the dough in it. Set aside to rise.

7. When risen, roll the dough into golf sized balls.

8. Arrange on a cookie sheet and set aside to rise again.

9. Use the palm of your hand to flatten each dough ball.

10. Top each flattened ball with your filling of choice and set aside to rise a final time.

11. Preheat main oven to 375 degrees F.

12. Place the kolaches in the oven and bake for 16-18 minutes. Allow to cool before serving.

Nevada - Frank's Clams Posillipo

Nevada may not have any dishes of its own, but it does have Frank Sinatra's favorite clam recipe. The crooner helped to transform Las Vegas from a desert town to a glittering hub of entertainment, and so it's only right that Clam Posillipo represents the Silver State.

Portions: 4

Prep Time: **10mins**

Total Time: **50mins**

Ingredients:

- 32 littleneck clams
- 3 tbsp. virgin olive oil
- 6 cloves garlic (sliced in half)
- ¼ cup yellow onion (finely chopped)
- 28 ounces canned whole plum tomatoes with juice
- Sea salt and freshly ground black pepper
- 1 tbsp. tomato paste
- ¼ cup fresh basil (chopped)
- 1 tbsp. flat leaf parsley (chopped)

- Parsley (to garnish)

Directions:

1. Using a brush, scrub the littleneck clams, and rinse under running cold tap water.

2. Transfer the scrubbed clams to a large pan or pot, covering with sufficient cold water to just cover. Over high heat, bring to boil, boiling until for 4-5 minutes, or until the clams open. Discard any unopened clams.

3. Using a slotted spoon, remove the opened clams from the pot and place in a bowl.

4. Using a coffee filter, line a strainer and pour the clam cooking water through the strainer. Set a ¾ cup of this liquid aside, you will need it to prepare the broth.

5. Put the clams back in the pot, adding water and swirl to remove any debris or sand. Drain the clams and return them to the bowl.

6. Over moderate heat, and in a large pan, heat the olive oil. When hot, fry the garlic for 2 minutes, or until browned and fragrant.

7. Using kitchen tongs, remove the garlic from the pan and discard.

8. Add the chopped onion to the pan and sauté in the garlic infused oil for a few minutes, or until just soft.

9. Using a wooden spoon, break the tomatoes up and add the tomatoes along with the juice to the pan.

10. Bring to boil, reducing the heat, cover and simmer for 20-25 minutes, occasionally stirring.

11. Taste the sauce and season. Add the tomato paste and stir to incorporate.

12. Add ¼ cup of basil and the chopped parsley.

13. Simmer, for 4-5 minutes. Do not cover the pan.

14. Pour in the clam broth set aside earlier to the sauce and boil.

15. Cover the pan with a lid, and reduce the heat to a simmer, simmering for 7-10 minutes, or until the clams are sufficiently cooked.

16. Ladle the clams along with the sauce into individual bowls, garnish with chopped parsley and serve with crusty baguette.

New Hampshire - Seafood Chowder With Lobster

Along its beautiful, albeit brief Atlantic coast, New Hampshire has an abundance of seafood. The state has a long tradition of sourcing local foods.

Here, you will find food prepared just as it was in the 18th century.

Portions: 12-15

Prep Time: **25mins**

Total Time: 1hour 25mins

Ingredients:

- 3 (1 pound) lobsters
- 3 cups red potatoes (unpeeled, chopped into ¼" cubes)
- 4 slices thick bacon (finely chopped)
- 4 tbsp. salted butter
- 2 ribs celery (chopped into ¼" cubes)

- 1 medium yellow onion (peeled, chopped into ¼" cubes)
- ¼ cup all-purpose flour
- 2 cups light cream
- ½ cup clam juice
- 1 pound bay scallops
- 1 pound clam meat, fresh with juices (chopped)
- 1 pound small shrimp
- 1½ pounds filleted haddock (skinned, chopped into 1" pieces)
- 1 cup whole milk
- 1 tsp kosher salt
- White pepper
- Paprika (to serve)

Directions:

1. Set a large lobster pot, filled halfway with cold water, over a high heat and bring lobsters to fast boil.

2. Put the lobsters in the pot, reducing the temperature to moderate and cooking for 8 minutes.

3. Remove the lobsters from the pot and put to one side for cooling. Set 4½ cups of the cooking water to one side.

4. Once the lobsters have cooled enough to easily handle, remove the meat from the tails, claws and claw joint. Coarsely chop the lobster meat and put to one side.

5. Pour 4 cups of lobster water set aside earlier into a 3-4 quart pot, add the red potatoes, and simmer for 5-

7 minutes, or until just tender. Drain the lobster and put to one side.

6. In a large skillet or frying pan, fry the diced bacon, occasionally turning, for 8-10 minutes, or until cooked through but not crispy. Set the bacon to one side.

7. Over moderate to low heat and using a 5-quart pot, melt the butter.

8. Add the celery along with the onion and cook while continually stirring for 6-8 minutes, or until the vegetables are just tender.

9. Add the cooked bacon and continue cooking for another 2-3 minutes.

10. Gradually, add in the flour, continually whisking, to make a roux.

11. Turn the heat down to low and stir for a further 4-5 minutes.

12. Increasing the heat to moderate add the remaining lobster water, while slowly whisking. Next, add the cream and the clam juice. Whisking to combine.

13. Add the bay scallops together with the clam meat and its juice, the shrimp and the haddock.

14. Add the cooked red potatoes, and milk. Stir to combine and season with salt and white pepper.

15. Reduce heat to a simmer and stir until all of the fish is cooked, around 15-20 minutes.

16. When you are ready to serve, stir in the cooked lobster meat.

17. Garnish with paprika and serve.

New Jersey - Chinese Beef With Jersey Tomatoes

Famous for its juicy, sweet, red tomatoes, the Garden State of Jersey has the sixth largest Chinese population in the United States. This recipe marries East with West.

Portions: 4

Prep Time: **10mins**

Total Time: **45mins**

Ingredients:

Marinade:

- 1 tbsp. soy sauce
- 1 tbsp. dry sherry
- 1 tsp cornstarch
- 1 pound beef sirloin (sliced into 2" strips, ¼" thick)

Sauce:

- 2 tbsp. Worcestershire sauce
- ½ tbsp. soy sauce
- ½ tbsp. dry sherry
- 1-2 tbsp. corn oil
- 1 whole onion (peeled, sliced)
- 3 cloves garlic (chopped)
- 1 pound ripe Jersey tomatoes (cut into wedges)
- Jasmine rice (steamed, to serve)

Directions:

1. First, marinate the strips of beef.

2. In a small mixing bowl, combine the soy sauce with 1 tablespoon of dry sherry, and cornstarch. Blend until incorporated and add to the strips of beef, tossing well to combine. Cover the bowl, and transfer to the refrigerator to marinate for 30 minutes.

3. Next, prepare the sauce. In a small mixing bowl, combine the Worcestershire sauce, along with the soy sauce and sherry, stir to combine and put to one side.

4. Over a moderate heat and in a large skillet or wok, add the corn oil. When hot, add the sliced onions and chopped garlic and stir-fry for 30-40 seconds until fragrant and just soft.

5. Add the Jersey tomatoes to the skillet and cook for 2-3 minutes, until soft but firm.

6. Pour the sauce into the skillet and mix to combine. Add the slices of beef and stir-fry for 1-2 minutes until cooked through.

7. Serve with steamed jasmine rice.

New Mexico - Green Chili Apple Pie

Whether sweet or savory, chilies feature heavily in New Mexico cuisine; from mains to desserts New Mexicans can't get enough of them.

Portions: 8-10

Prep Time: **15mins**

Total Time: 9hours 5mins

Ingredients:

Crust:

- 4 tbsp. lard (chopped into ½" cubes)
- 2 cups all-purpose flour + additional for dusting
- 1 tbsp. white sugar
- 1 tsp sea salt
- 1 tsp baking powder
- Ice water

Filling:

- 7 Granny Smith apples (peeled and sliced)

- ½ cup all-purpose flour
- ½ cup turbinado sugar + additional for sprinkling
- 2 tbsp. ground cinnamon
- ½ tsp ground ginger
- ½ tsp fresh nutmeg (grated)
- ¼ cup freshly squeezed lemon juice
- ¼ cup canned chopped hot green chilies
- ¼ cup pine nuts
- 1 egg
- Vanilla ice cream

Directions:

1. Freeze the cubed lard for 60 minutes.

2. In a large mixing bowl, combine the flour along with the white sugar, sea salt, and baking powder.

3. Using 2 kitchen knives, cut in the lard, until a coarse, pea size, consistency is achieved; taking care not to over mix.

4. Gradually, stir in between ½-1 cup of ice water; the dough needs to hold well together when squeezed.

5. Divide the dough evenly between 2 pieces of plastic wrap, using the wrap to form each half piece into a disk shape. Wrap the dough tightly and place in the fridge until firm; 4-6 hours.

6. Next, make the filling. In a large mixing bowl combine the apples along with the flour, turbinado sugar, ground cinnamon, ginger, grated nutmeg, fresh

lemon juice, green chilies and pine nuts. Put to one side to rest for 20 minutes.

7. Preheat the main oven to 375 degrees F.

8. Roll out 1 dough disk into a 12" round on a clean, lightly floured work surface. Ease the round into a deep (9") pie plate.

9. Spoon the filling into the pie crust.

10. Roll out the remaining dough disk into a 12" circle and lay it on top of the filling.

11. Gently, press the crusts to one another, fold the overhanging dough under itself and using your fingers, crimp the edges.

12. Cut 3 or 4 slits into the top of the crust or prick with a metal fork, this will allow steam to escape.

13. Whisk the egg along with ¼ cup water and lightly brush it over the top.

14. Sprinkle the top of the pie with a little sugar.

15. Bake the pie in the oven, rotating the pie every 16-18 minutes, until golden; for between 60-90 minutes.

16. Allow the pie to cool before serving with vanilla ice cream.

New York – Classic Baked Vanilla Cheesecake

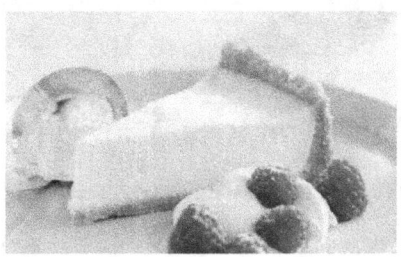

Cakes made of soft cheese may very well date back to ancient Greece, but it was American dairyman, William Lawrence of Chester in New York who created what would become New York cheesecake.

William, in trying to mimic the French Neufchatel cheese, stumbled upon a creamier, richer and un-ripened cheese and it is this cream cheese that was to become the basis for this simple yet iconic dessert.

Portions: 12

Prep Time: **40mins**

Total Time: 7hours 35mins

Ingredients:

- 1½ cups graham cracker crumbs
- ¼ cup white sugar
- ⅓ cup butter (melted)
- 3 (8ounce) packages cream cheese (room temperature)

- 1½ cups white sugar (divided)
- 4 medium eggs (room temperature)
- 1 tbsp. + 1 tsp vanilla extract (divided)
- 1 tsp cream of tartar
- 1-pint sour cream

Directions:

1. Preheat the main oven to 350 degrees F.

2. In a mixing bowl, combine the cracker crumbs along with the sugar and butter and stir until evenly moist.

3. Gently, press the crumb mixture into the bottom, and ½" up the sides of a springform (9") pan.

4. In a large mixing bowl, and using an electric mixer, mix the cream cheese with the sugar until silky smooth. Add the eggs, and blend in 1 tablespoon of vanilla extract, and cream of tartar. Pour the mixture over the pie crust.

5. Bake in the preheated oven until the middle is set, around 45-50 minutes. Put to one side to cool for 5 minutes.

6. In a medium bowl, mix the sour cream with 1 teaspoon of vanilla and ½ cup sugar, until silky smooth. Carefully pour the mixture over the cheesecake working from the sides of the springform pan towards the middle.

7. Return to the oven for a further 5 minutes.

8. Allow the cheesecake to cool in the pan at room temperature.

9. Transfer to the fridge for a minimum of 5-6 hours before serving.

North Carolina - Sweet Potato Pie

It's only natural that North Carolina, as the top US sweet potato producer, should make the best sweet potato pie. Did you know that what we now think of as delicious dessert was once breakfast for the fisherman of days gone by?

Portions: 8

Prep Time: **10mins**

Total Time: **1hour**

Ingredients:

- 2¼ cups cooked mashed sweet potatoes
- ¾ cup granulated sugar
- ½ cup firmly packed brown sugar
- ½ cup instant French vanilla pudding mix
- ¾ cup evaporated milk
- 2 large eggs (room temperature)
- 6 tbsp. butter (softened)
- 1 teaspoon ground cinnamon

- 1½ tbsp. vanilla extract
- 1 (9") unbaked pie shell
- Whipped cream (to garnish)

Directions:

1. In a large mixing bowl combine the first 9 ingredients and beat at moderate speed until well blended. Evenly spread the mixture into the unbaked pie shell.

2. Bake at 450 degrees F for 10 minutes before reducing to 350 degrees F and baking for a further 40 minutes or until the pie is firm.

3. Cool before serving on a wire baking rack.

4. Garnish with whipped cream.

North Dakota - Knoephla Soup

Knoephla, or potato dumpling soup, is a traditional North Dakotan dish taken to the US by German immigrants from Russia. A hearty, comforting soup typically made from dumplings, potatoes, onions and fresh chopped parsley.

Portions: 6

Prep Time: **5mins**

Total Time: **30mins**

Ingredients:

- 1½ cups all-purpose flour
- 1 tsp baking powder
- ¼ tsp salt
- 1 medium egg (lightly beaten)
- ½ cup whole milk
- 2 tbsp. cooking oil
- 3½ cups chicken stock
- 1 (1.8 ounce) white sauce mix
- 4 medium potatoes (chopped)

- 1 large onion (chopped)
- 1 cup cooked ham (diced)
- 1 (12 ounce) can evaporated milk
- ½ tsp ground white pepper
- ¼ cup fresh parsley (snipped)

Directions:

1. To make the dumplings, in a large bowl, combine the flour, baking powder, and salt. Stir well to incorporate. Make a well in the middle of the flour mixture.

2. In a small bowl, combine the egg, along with the milk and oil. Add this to the flour and mix to incorporate. Cover the bowl and set to one side.

3. For the soup. In a 4-5 quart Dutch oven, a little at a time, add the broth into the sauce mix, stirring, until a smooth consistency. Add the potatoes, onion, diced ham, evaporated milk and white pepper. Stir well.

4. Bring to the boil, reduce heat to a simmer and cover with a lid, simmer while occasionally stirring for 15 minutes.

5. Drop rounded heaped teaspoons of the dough mixture into the soup. Bring back to the boil, before reducing to a simmer.

6. Continue simmering, uncovered for 12-15 minutes, or until the potatoes are fork tender.

7. Garnish with parsley.

Ohio - Buckeyes

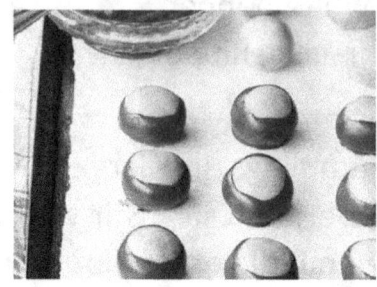

Ohio is known as the Buckeye State, mainly because lots of buckeye trees once covered the state's hills and plains.

Originally though, the name Buckeye comes from the Native American Indians, who named the nut hetuck (buckeye) because the nut's marking looks very much like the eye of a deer.

Looking very much like peanut butter balls, buckeye candy is hugely popular in Ohio.

Portions: 40-50 balls

Prep Time: **10mins**

Total Time: 4hours 30mins

Ingredients:

- 1½ cups peanut butter
- ½ cup butter
- 1 pound powdered sugar
- 1 tsp vanilla

- 1½ cups milk chocolate chips
- Shortening

Directions:

1. In a mixing bowl, combine the peanut butter, butter, powdered sugar, and vanilla and stir to incorporate.

2. Shape the mixture into 1" balls and place in the refrigerator.

3. In the meantime, using a double boiler, melt the chocolate along with a little shortening; to enable the chocolate to harden.

4. Insert a cocktail stick into the refrigerated balls and dip into the melted chocolate, leaving a small area uncoated, to resemble a Buckeye.

5. Cool the Buckeyes on parchment paper and store in the fridge.

Oklahoma - Chicken-Fried Steak And Gravy

Nearly 30 years ago Oklahoma state legislature placed chicken fried steak on the official State Meal list. Crispy, juicy center served with a creamy based gravy, and a side of mashed potatoes is the order of the day.

Portions: 4

Prep Time: **15mins**

Total Time: **35mins**

Ingredients:

- 1¼ cups all purpose flour (divided)
- 2 large eggs
- 1½ cups skim milk (divided)
- 4 (6 ounce) beef cube steaks
- 1¼ tsp salt (divided)
- 1 tsp pepper (divided)
- Oil
- 1 cup cold water

Directions:

1. Put 1 cup of flour into a shallow mixing bowl. Whisk the eggs together with ½ cup milk until incorporated. Sprinkle each of the steaks with ¾ teaspoon each of salt and pepper.

2. Dip the steaks in flour to evenly coat on both sides, shaking off any excess flour. Dip the steaks in the egg-milk mixture and then again in the flour.

3. In a large frying pan or skillet, heat ¼" of oil over moderate heat. Add the steaks, and cook for 4-6 minutes, on both sides until golden; a thermometer should read 160 degrees F.

4. Remove the steak from the pan and drain on kitchen paper towels. Keep the steaks warm.

5. Remove all except 2 tablespoons of oil from the frying pan.

6. Add the remaining flour (¼ cup), ½ teaspoon salt and ¼ teaspoon of black pepper and stir until silky smooth. Continue cooking over moderate heat for 4 minutes, or until golden.

7. A little at a time add the cold water and any remaining milk. Bring to a swift boil, continually stirring, and cook and stir for a couple of minutes until thickened.

8. Serve the gravy with the chicken fried steaks along with a side of mashed potatoes.

Oregon - Marionberry Cream Cheese Pie

Oregon is one of the very few marionberry fruit producers and what better way to showcase this sweet, and tart fruit than with a delicious pie?

The king of blackberries is perfect for ice cream, tarts, pies and all manner of desserts.

Portions: 8

Prep Time: **20mins**

Total Time: **2hours**

Ingredients:
- 2 cups all-purpose flour
- 1 tbsp. sugar
- 1 tsp salt
- ½ cup cold butter (cubed)
- 5 tbsp. shortening
- 4 tbsp. ice water

- 2 tbsp. lemon juice

Filling:
- 1 cup + 1 tsp sugar (divided)
- 2 tbsp. + 2 tsp quick-cooking tapioca
- 1 tbsp. lemon juice
- 4 cups fresh marionberries
- 1 package (8 ounces) cream cheese (softened)
- ½ cup confectioners' sugar
- ½ tsp almond extract
- ½ tsp vanilla extract
- 1 tbsp. heavy whipping cream

Directions:

1. In a large mixing bowl, combine the flour along with the sugar and salt. Mix well. Add, and cut in the cubes of butter and shortening until a crumbly consistency.

2. A little at a time, add the ice water along with the 1 tbsp. of lemon juice, toss with a fork until the dough holds well together when pressed.

3. Divide the dough into 2 pieces.

4. Using clean hands, form each piece into a disk shape, wrap in plastic wrap and transfer to the refrigerator for 10 minutes.

5. In the meanwhile, using a large mixing bowl, add 1 cup of sugar, together with the tapioca and lemon juice.

6. Add the marionberries, tossing to coat and allow to rest for 15 minutes.

7. Preheat the main oven to 425 degrees F.

8. On a lightly floured, clean surface, roll one half of the dough into a ⅛" thick circle, and place on a 9" round pie plate. Trim the pastry to overlap the plate rim by ½".

9. In a small mixing bowl, beat the softened cream cheese, confectioners' sugar, almond extract, and vanilla extract. Top with the marionberry mixture.

10. Roll out the remaining dough to a circle of no more than 1/8" thick, and cut into strips approximately ½" wide.

11. Arrange the strips over the fruit filling in a lattice design.

12. Trim and seal the strips to the edge of the pastry and crimp and flute.

13. Brush the strips with cream and scatter over any remaining sugar.

14. Bake in the oven for 15 minutes, before reducing the heat to 350 degrees F.

15. Bake for a further 50-60 minutes or until the filling bubbles and the crust becomes golden.

16. Cool down on a wire baking rack before servings.

Pennsylvania - Root Beer Beef Stew

While on his honeymoon, a pharmacist from Philadelphia, Charles Hires discovered a recipe for herbal tea. He began selling a dry version of the mixture while started work on a liquid equivalent.

The result of this hard work, root beer, was introduced in 1876 at the Philadelphia Centennial Exhibitions.

Portions: 8

Prep Time: **20mins**

Total Time: 4hours 20mins

Ingredients:

- 3 tbsp. olive oil
- Salt and pepper
- 2 pounds beef stew meat (cubed)
- 1 medium onion (diced)
- 3 cloves garlic minced
- 12 ounces root beer
- 3½ cups beef broth

- 2 tbsp. tomato paste
- 1 tbsp. Worcestershire sauce
- ½ tsp paprika
- 8 new potatoes (quartered, chopped)
- 4 carrots (sliced diagonally)
- 3 tbsp. all-purpose flour
- Fresh parsley (finely chopped)

Directions:

1. In a large pan or Dutch oven, over moderate to high heat, heat the olive oil.

2. Season the meat; add to the pan, browning on all sides. Remove the meat to a plate.

3. Add the onion to the pan and reduce heat to low. Continue cooking until softened, for between 3-4 minutes.

4. Add the garlic and cook for a further 60 seconds.

5. Pour in the root beer, together with the beef broth, tomato paste, Worcestershire sauce, paprika, ½ tsp salt, and pinch pepper. Return the beef to the pot and simmer until the beef is tender, for between 1½ - 2hours.

6. Stir in the chopped potatoes and carrots and simmer until the veggies are just tender and the meat falls apart, between 30-45 minutes.

7. Remove 1 cup of liquid from the pot and add the flour, slowly whisking.

8. Gradually, stir the flour mixture back into the pot and slowly bring to boil.

9. Reduce the heat and simmer for 8-10 minutes, or until thickened.

10. Taste, and adjust the seasoning.

11. Garnish with parsley.

Rhode Island - Baked Apples And Sausage

The crisp, sharp greening apple is Rhode Island's official state fruit and it perfect not just for sweet pies but also for savory dishes.

Portions: 6

Prep Time: **15mins**

Total Time: **55mins**

Ingredients:
- 1 pound bulk sausage
- 6 Rhode Island Greening apples
- 2 tbsp. brown sugar
- 1 tsp ground cinnamon
- ¼ tsp lemon rind (grated)

Directions:

1. In a large frying pan or skillet brown the sausages.

2. Wash the apples, cut off the tops, remove the apple cores and hollow out the apples, leaving a ½" thickness. Set the apple flesh aside.

3. Take the apple flesh and combine with the browned sausage, sugar, cinnamon and grated lemon, stir to combine.

4. Fill each of the apples with the sausage mixture.

5. Transfer the filled apples to a casserole dish, cover, and bake in the oven at 375 degrees F, for around 40 minutes, or until tender.

South Carolina - Old Charleston Style Shrimp And Grits

Once served primarily due to economic considerations, this traditional breakfast dish is becoming more upscale.

Grits have a deep-rooted Southern history and this combination of locally sourced and abundant shrimp combined with grits is a popular soul food staple.

Portions: 8

Prep Time: **30mins**

Total Time: 1hour 15mins

Ingredients:

- 3 cups water
- 1 cup coarsely ground grits
- 2 tsp salt
- 2 cups half and half
- Salt (to taste)

- 2 pounds uncooked shrimp (peeled, deveined)
- 1 pinch cayenne pepper
- 1 lemon (juiced)
- 1 pound andouille sausage (cut into ¼" slices)
- 5 slices bacon
- 1 red bell pepper (chopped)
- 1 green bell pepper (chopped)
- 1 yellow bell pepper (chopped)
- 1 cup onion (chopped)
- 1 tsp garlic (minced)
- ¼ cup butter
- ¼ cup all-purpose flour
- 1 cup chicken broth
- 1 tbsp. Worcestershire sauce
- 1 cup sharp Cheddar cheese (shredded)

Directions:

1. In a heavy, large saucepan complete with lid bring the water, grits, and salt to boiling point.

2. Add the half and half and stir to combine; simmer for 15-20 minutes, or until the grits are just tender and beginning to thicken. Set to one side while keeping warm.

3. Sprinkle salt over the shrimp along with cayenne pepper and drizzle with lemon juice. Set to one side in a mixing bowl.

4. Arrange the slices of sausages in a large frying pan or skillet and over moderate heat, fry for 6-8 minutes, or until brown. Remove the frying pan from the heat.

5. In a skillet, over moderate to high heat, fry the bacon, occasionally turning, until the bacon is evenly browned, around 10 minutes. Reserve the bacon drippings in the skillet. Place the cooked bacon onto kitchen paper, and allow to cool; once cool, crumble the bacon.

6. Add the red, green and yellow peppers, along with the onion and garlic, to the bacon drippings until the onion is softened and translucent; cook while stirring for 6-8 minutes.

7. Add the shrimp and the cooked veggies to the andouille sausage and stir to incorporate.

8. In a medium saucepan over moderate heat, melt the butter. When melted, stir in the flour to make a paste. Reduce the heat to low and while continually stirring, cook until the mixture is brown 8-10 minutes. Take care not to burn the mixture.

9. Transfer the butter and flour mixture to the sausage, shrimp, and veggies in the skillet. Place the skillet over moderate heat and pour in the broth together with the bacon and Worcestershire sauce, continually stirring, while cooking until the sauce begins to thicken and the shrimp is opaque and vivid pink, around 6-8 minutes.

10. When you are ready to serve, mix the grated Cheddar into the grits and stir until the cheese melts, and the grits become pale yellow and creamy.

11. Serve the shrimp mixture over the Cheddar cheese grits.

South Dakota – Kuchen

The German word for cake, kuchen, is the designated official state dessert of South Dakota. This wedding dessert was brought to the USA by German immigrants from Russia in the late 19th century.

Although typically consisting of sweet dough with custard filling, during the Great Depression, hungry families filled it with cottage cheese or even onions.

Portions: 8

Prep Time: **15mins**

Total Time: 1hour 35mins

Ingredients:

For the dough:
- 2 cups milk (warm)
- ½ cup sugar
- 1 (14 ounce) package yeast
- 6 cups flour
- ½ cup oil

- 1 tsp salt
- 2 medium eggs

Filling:

- 1-quart heavy cream
- 6 medium eggs
- 1 cup sugar
- Dash salt
- Fruit (for topping)
- Cinnamon-sugar mixture

Directions:

1. In a mixing bowl, combine all the dough ingredients and mix well.

2. Using clean hands mold the dough into one sizeable ball and transfer to a well oiled mixing bowl. Cover the bowl and set aside at room temperature to enable the dough to rise and double in size.

3. In the meantime, and while the dough rises, combine the first 4 filling ingredients in a small sized pan and over moderate heat, cook while stirring until thickened. Set to one side to cool.

4. Next, prepare your favorite fruit.

5. Divide the dough mixture into even sized ball shapes and roll to fit into pie pans.

6. Arrange the fruit on top of the add and add the filling (approximately ½ cup per kuchen)

7. Sprinkle sugar and cinnamon over the top (1:1 ratio).

8. Bake in the oven at 350 degrees F for 18-20 minutes.

9. The custard filling will begin to set once the kuchen cools.

Tennessee - Elvis Presley's Baked Ham In Cola

One of the King's favorite dishes represents this beautiful and soulful state.

Portions: 12

Prep Time: **5mins**

Total Time: 1hour 45mins

Ingredients:

- 1 tbsp. mustard
- 1 can pineapple rings (drained, retain juice)
- 1 cup molasses
- 1 (11 ounce) can cola
- 6-pound ham

Directions:

1. Preheat the main oven to 400 degrees F.

2. In a mixing bowl, combine the mustard along with the pineapple rings and juice, molasses and cola.

3. Add the ham to a roasting pan.

4. Baste the ham with the mustard-cola glaze and bake in the oven, while remembering to continue basting every 15 minutes.

5. Bake until cooked through and in accordance with the directions on package.

Texas - Beef Chili Con Carne

Texas style chili is one of the most popular dishes in Texas. So much so, that 40 years ago it was designated as the Lone Star state's official dish. And you know what they say; don't mess with Texas.

Portions: 4-5

Prep Time: **30mins**

Total Time: 1hour 55mins

Ingredients:
- 4 pounds boneless chuck roast (cut into ½" pieces)
- 2 tbsp. chili powder
- 2 (6 ounce) cans tomato paste
- 1 (32 ounce) container beef broth
- 2 (8 ounce) cans tomato sauce
- 2 tsp granulated garlic
- 1 tsp salt
- 1 tsp ground oregano
- 1 tsp onion powder
- 1 tsp paprika

- ½ tsp ground black pepper
- 1 tsp ground cumin
- ¼ tsp ground red pepper
- Cornbread sticks (optional)
- Tortilla chips, sour cream, shredded cheese (optional)

Directions:

1. Over moderate to high heat, in a Dutch oven, brown the meat.

2. Remove the meat, reserving the meat drippings in the Dutch oven.

3. Add the chili powder and cook, continually stirring for 2-3 minutes.

4. Add the tomato paste, and stir, cooking for 5 minutes.

5. Return the beef to the Dutch oven, and add the beef broth, while stirring, along with the next 9 ingredients (tomato sauce through red pepper). Bring to boil.

6. Reduce the heat and uncovered, simmer while occasionally stirring, for 90 minutes, or until the beef is tender.

7. Serve with cornbread and your choice of toppings.

Utah - Sweet Onion Soup

Onions have been grown on the plains of Salt Lake Valley for generations, and in 2002, the Spanish Sweet Onion was designated Utah's state vegetable.

Portions: 2-4

Prep Time: **10mins**

Total Time: **25mins**

Ingredients:

- 5 cups sweet onions (sliced)
- ½ cup butter
- 1 tbsp. flour
- 4 cups beef broth
- ½-1 tsp sugar*
- Salt and pepper to taste
- French bread (toasted)
- Cheddar cheese (to garnish)

Directions:

1. In a large pot, sauté the onions in butter over a low heat until they are just tender, and beginning to brown on the edges.

2. Sprinkle the flour over the onions and continue cooking for 1-2 minutes.

3. Add the broth, sugar, salt, and pepper and while stirring, cook over moderate heat for a further 10 minutes.

4. Ladle the soup into ovenproof bowls.

5. Place one slice of toasted French bread on the top of each bowl and sprinkle with grated cheese.

6. Cook in the oven until the cheese begins to melt.

*The amount of sugar will depend on the sweetness of the onions.

Vermont - Maple Syrup Pork Chops

Naturally, as the nation's leading maple syrup producer Vermont proudly presents tender pork chops in a maple syrup infused sauce.

Portions: 4

Prep Time: **5mins**

Total Time: **25mins**

Ingredients:

- 4 medium-large, 1" thick, pork chops
- Salt
- 2 tbsp. butter
- ¼ cup onion (minced)
- 1 tbsp. apple cider vinegar
- 1 tsp chili powder
- ½ tsp pepper
- ¼ cup maple syrup
- 2 tbsp. Worcestershire sauce
- Oil

- 1 medium onion sliced (sliced onion optional)
- 1 tbsp. flour (to thicken)

Directions:

1. Preheat the main oven to 400 degrees F.

2. Sprinkle both sides of the chops with a dash of salt.

3. In a large frying pan, over moderate to high heat, heat the butter.

4. Pat each chop dry, using kitchen paper towels and transfer to the frying pan. Fry, without moving, to sufficiently brown, flip the chops over and brown on the reverse side.

5. Take the chops out of the pan and transfer to a roasting pan, with high sides.

6. To make the sauce. Add the onion to the pan and sauté for a few minutes, until the onions browns. Add the cider vinegar along with the chili powder, pepper, and maple syrup and Worcestershire sauce, bring to boil.

7. Pour the sauce, evenly over the pork chops in the roasting pan.

8. Lower the oven temperature to 350 degrees F and bake in the oven for between 10-15 minutes, or until cooked through. There is no need to cover the pan.

9. Using the pan you used for the sauce, add a drop of oil and heat to moderate. Cook the onions, scraping up any sauce left in the pan. Cook until gently browned. You can do this while the chops are in the oven, baking.

10. Place the chops on a serving plate and tent, loosely with aluminum foil.

11. Pour the sauce into the pan used for the chops and add 1 tablespoon of flour, whisk.

12. Season with salt.

13. Pour the gravy over the pork chops and onions.

Virginia - Cream Of Peanut Soup

A southern delicacy, peanut soup dates back to the 1700s. It is said that peanuts were brought to the USA by Portuguese slave traders who gave them to slaves in transit from the Africa.

Portions: 10-12

Prep Time: **10mins**

Total Time: 1hour 10mins

Ingredients:

- ½ stick unsalted butter
- 1 medium onion (finely chopped)
- 2 celery ribs (finely chopped)
- 3 tbsp. flour
- 8 cups chicken stock
- 2 cups smooth peanut butter
- 1¾ cups light cream
- Salted peanuts (finely chopped)

Directions:

1. In a large soup pan over moderate heat, melt the butter. Add the chopped onion along with the celery and cook, while stirring, until just soft, for 35 minutes.

2. Stir in the flour and cook for a further 2 minutes.

3. Pour in the stock and increase the heat to high, and bring to boil, continually stirring.

4. Reduce the heat to moderate and cook, stirring, until the mixture slightly reduces and thickens, for 15 minutes.

5. Pour the mixture into a sieve set over a large bowl and strain, while pushing down hard on the solids to extract the maximum flavor. Return the liquid to the pot.

6. In a bowl, whisk the peanut butter along with the cream into the liquid.

7. Over a low heat, warm, while whisking, for 5 minutes. Do not allow the mixture to boil.

8. Serve the soup warm and garnish with peanuts.

Washington - Chili Half-Smokes

A local sausage delicacy, a half-smoke, is larger and spicier than a hot dog. Smoked and served with chili sauce and onions, this is a hugely popular dish in Washington.

Portions: 8

Prep Time: **10mins**

Total Time: **45mins**

Ingredients

Sauce:

- 12 ounces beef chuck (finely ground)
- 1 yellow onion (finely chopped)
- 3 tbsp. chili powder
- 1 tsp mustard powder
- Sea salt
- ¼ tsp ground cumin
- ½ tsp ground coriander
- ⅛ tsp cayenne pepper
- 1 bay leaf

- 1 garlic cloves (minced)
- ¼ cup tomato paste
- 2 tbsp. apple cider vinegar
- 1½ tbsp. canola oil
- 2 tbsp. all-purpose flour
- 2 cups chicken broth

Hot Dogs:

- 8 half-smoke hot dogs (regular size)
- ¼ cup yellow mustard
- 8 split-top hot dog buns (toasted)
- ½ cup white onion (diced)

Directions:

1. First make the sauce. Over moderate heat, place a large frying pan and sauté the beef along with the chopped onions, 1 tbsp. chili powder, mustard powder, 1 tsp kosher salt, cumin, coriander, cayenne, bay leaf and minced garlic. Cook for 7-8 minutes, using the back of a wooden spoon to break up the beef.

2. Slide the meat mixture to one half of the pan and to the empty side of the pan, add the tomato paste, while cooking and stirring until the paste thickens, around 2-3 minutes. Add the paste to the meat and cook for a further 2 minutes.

3. Add the cider vinegar, ensuring that any brown bits stuck to the pan are scraped up using a wooden spoon, and cook for a further couple of minutes.

4. In the meantime, heat the oil in another large frying pan or skillet over moderate heat.

5. Add the remaining 2 tablespoons of chili powder and the flour and using a wooden spoon, mix until silky and toasted, for 1-2 minutes.

6. Add the chicken broth, while whisking, continuing to cook until thickened.

7. Increase the heat to moderate to high and simmer until the mixture reduces by 25%; ideally a yield of around 1½ cups, for 4-5 minutes.

8. Pour over the meat mixture, and simmer while stirring until incorporated, 1-2 minutes. Remove and discard the bay leaf and season well with salt.

9. For the hot dogs. Preheat a grill to high.

10. Cut the half-smokes ¾ of the way through lengthwise and grill until marked and sufficiently heated, for around 1½ minutes each side.

11. Spread a little mustard on each bun. Transfer each half-smoke to a bun and top with chili sauce and raw onions.

West Virginia - Barbecued Bear

Hunting is of great importance in the state of West Virginia where it is responsible for creating more than 5000 jobs. Every year, hundreds of thousands of hunters take to the woods in search of game.

Portions: 4-6

Prep Time: **20mins**

Total Time: 2hours 30mins

Ingredients:

- 3 pounds bear steak
- 2 tbsp. vegetable oil
- 1 cup ketchup
- 2 tbsp. tarragon vinegar
- 1 large onion (peeled, diced)
- 1 tbsp. chili powder
- 1/3 cup steak sauce
- 1 tbsp. lemon juice
- ½ tsp salt

Directions:

1. First, trim the bear steak from all its fat and cut into 2" cubes.

2. In a frying pan or skillet heat the oil. Add the bear to the pan and brown on all sides.

3. Transfer the browned meat to a casserole dish.

4. Add the remaining 7 ingredients to the frying pan and bring to boil, continually stirring.

5. Pour the sauce over the meat in the casserole dish. Cover the dish and bake in the oven at 325 degrees F, for a minimum of 2 hours, or until tender, occasionally stirring.

6. The meat needs to be well done before serving.

Wisconsin - Beer Brats

Bratwurst or beer brats is a type of German sausage made from beef, veal or pork. Wisconsin is home to the beer brat and a result of German immigrants. Today, it is an American classic.

Portions: 12

Prep Time: **5mins**

Total Time: **30mins**

Ingredients:

- 12 uncooked bratwurst sausages
- 2 cans beer
- 1 onion (thinly sliced)
- 12 brat buns
- Ketchup

Directions:

1. In a deep pan over moderate to high heat, add the bratwurst and barely cover with beer. Add the onion and stir.

2. Bring to boil, reduce the heat, and simmer until the sausages are cooked through; this will take between 15-20 minutes.

3. Transfer the sausage to a bowl and drain off the beer, returning the sausages to the pan.

4. Increase the heat to moderate and cook the sausages, while frequently turning, for about 5 minutes.

5. Serve in brat buns with a generous dollop of ketchup.

Wyoming - Tenderloin Of Beef

The Cowboy State serves up some tasty old cowboy cuisine.

Portions: 6-8

Prep Time: **10mins**

Total Time: 1hour 20mins

Ingredients:

- 1 (4 pound) beef tenderloin (room temperature)
- 4 ounces bleu cheese (softened)
- ½ cup butter (softened)
- 1 tbsp. Worcestershire sauce
- 2 cloves garlic (crushed)

Directions:

1. Preheat the main oven to 450 degrees F.

2. Place the beef tenderloin on a roasting rack in a baking pan and transfer to the oven.

3. Reduce the oven temperature to 425 degrees F and roast for 20 minutes.

4. In a mixing bowl combine the bleu cheese, along with the butter, Worcestershire sauce, and garlic. Mix well to incorporate.

5. Reduce the oven temperature to 375 degrees F and roast for a further 10 minutes.

6. Spread the blue cheese sauce mixture over the beef and roast for another 30 -40 minutes, or until you achieve the desired degree of doneness.

Part 2

Introduction

There are tons of highly satiating and filling American recipes you can prepare in bulk for family and friends. These recipes give you the benefits of cooking your meals at home and also help you make the right choices of ingredients that will keep you healthy and well-nourished.

Preparing your meals at home will help you heat better and you can also make use of varieties of American-born recipes to create social bond, because social eating has become a staple trend in all American societies, whether you are from the North, East Coast, West Coast or the Southern region- you will always find delicious and highly nutritious meals that will cater for your needs.

By learning about different recipes, you will be able to make more informed choices and create your own new recipes. There are many traditional America recipes that are rich in food components such as lean protein, lean unsaturated fat, and essential vitamins and minerals, many of these recipes are even inspired by nature, and they appeal to every individual in the society.

The Thanksgiving Day is usually the time when many people become aware of the influence that Native American recipes have had in the world, but that is about to change as social eating becomes more popular all over the country. From the rich and colorful heart-friendly healthy foods such as pumpkin to the fiber-rich beans and anti-oxidant loaded berries, there are lots of American dishes you can relish to make your day filled with gratitude.

In our modern-day diets, it can be easy to overlook American fruits and veggies, the berries, for instance, grow wild across numerous parts of America, these include the blackberries, strawberries, raspberries, and blueberries and these fruits play so many parts in our native American diets. Berries are particularly rich in Vitamins, and minerals that help reduce the risks of stroke, and heart diseases. A cup of strawberries, for instance, contains the required daily dose of Vitamin C.

Mushrooms and pumpkins are also popular in American diets because they are nutrient-dense, and they contain Fiber, Potassium and Vitamin A that provides a wide range of benefits, even for those suffering from ailments such as diabetes. Beans are not only rich in fiber, they also contain cardiovascular health-boosting properties, they can be prepared with many American salads, soups, Tacos, chili and Burritos recipes.

There are too many other native foods that can be found in many American diets today and this book offers an insight into how you can optimize them in different diets without compromising your health.

Chapter 1: Healthy And Nutritious American Desserts Recipes

There are so many benefits attached to eating desserts. Consider how much few bites of dark chocolate a day can help reduce your risks of heart diseases, and stroke. From this chapter you can expect the following;

• Healthy desserts that you can consume for breakfast,

•A healthy chocolate dessert that can help you control blood pressure.

•Highly delicious recipes you can serve to your family and friends, especially during special occasions, and

• Delicious treats that will promote a positive mood, all day long.

Recipe #1: The Malt Hot Chocolate S'mores

This perhaps is one of the best chocolate recipes for vegetarians. Aside from offering great health benefits, it is one of those lovely desserts you can prepare under 5 minutes

Preparation time: 3 minutes
Servings: 8

Ingredients:

- 15-16 malted milk biscuits,
- 7-8 squares of milk chocolate,
- 8 vegetarian marshmallows

Direction

1. Pre-heat your grill to a high heat before lining a large baking sheet with a parchment paper. Add the malted milk biscuits unto a tray, and add the square of milk chocolate on 8 of the malted milk biscuits, then add the mash mallows on the remaining 8 of the malted milk chocolate. Grill them until they start to melt.
2. Sandwich the malted milk chocolates with the square of malted milk chocolate with those containing the mash mallows until the content in

the middle start to ooze at the edges, you can dunk them in extra chocolate for that extra chocolate flavor or eat them immediately after grilling hot.

Recipe #2: Brown Rice With Date And Carrot Puddings

Wonderful recipe for a special day.

Servings: 2-3

Preparation time: 30 minutes

Ingredients:

- ½ cup of fresh, chopped dates,
- 1 ½ cups of brown rice
- 2 teaspoons of non-fat dairy spread,
- 1 tablespoon of brown sugar,
- 1 medium to large size egg,
- 1 teaspoon of vanilla essence,
- 1 large grated carrot,
- 1 teaspoon of pure icing sugar.

Direction:

1. Pre-heat your oven to about 190 degrees, then grease some 4 (200mls) ramekins, and line the inner part of each with baking paper. Mix the dates inside half a cup of water, and heat over medium heat. Let the mix simmer for about 2 minutes and then set aside to cool. With the aid of an electric mixer, simply beat the sugar and spread until they are perfectly mixed.

2. Add the egg and vanilla essence and mi perfectly. Stir in the brown rice, carrot and date mix. Gently sift the flour over the date, and stir gently before using a spoon to pour it inside the ramekins, then place on the baking spray. Bake the mix for about 20 minutes, and let it stand for about 5 minutes before turning them in the serving plates. Serve immediately.

#3: Recipe #76: Apple Coffeecake

The wonderful taste of this cake makes it ideal for the young and old.

Preparation time: 11 minutes
Cooking time: 35 minutes
Servings: 20

Ingredients:

- 5 cups of tart, cored, peeled and chopped apples,
- 1 cup of brown sugar,
- 1 cup of dark raisins,
- ½ cup of chopped pecans,
- ¼ cup of vegetable oil,
- 2 teaspoons of vanilla,
- 1 cup of beaten egg
- 2 ½ cups of sifted, all-purpose flour,
- 1 ½ teaspoons of baking soda, and
- 2 teaspoons of ground cinnamon.

Direction:

1. Pre-heat the oven to about 450-degrees F, then lightly oil a 13x9x2 inches of baking pan (3 minutes).
2. In a large bowl, mix the apple with sugar, raisin, and pecans, and let the mix stand for about 5 minutes. (5 minutes)

3. Stir the mix inside oil, eggs, and vanilla then sifts together Cinnamon and baking soda, and flour. Stir this mix into the apple mix to moisten the final mix. (3 minutes)
4. Turn the batter into the pan and bake for about 34 minutes. Cool for few minutes and serve. (34 minutes).

Recipe #4: The Brownie Strawberry Trifle

Preparation time: 20 minutes

Servings: 6

Ingredients:

- 1 box of fudge brownie mix, alongside ingredients to make the brownies,
- 2 boxes of vanilla pudding,
- 1 ¾ cup of non-fat milk,
- 1 tub of whipped topping,
- 1 pint of strawberries,
- An optional chocolate bar, and
- Optional mint leaves.

Direction:

1. Bake the brownies according to instructions on the box, this should take about 15 minutes. (15 minutes)
2. Mix the vanilla pudding with the milk, then add the whipping topping, slice the strawberries. (5 minutes)
3. Inside the trifle bowl spread half of the brownies, alongside half of the pudding and whipping mix, as well as half of the strawberries. Shave the chocolate bar on top of the trifle as garnish and the optional mint leaves. Serve immediately. (10 minutes).

Chapter 2: The Very Delicious American Meaty Collections

Hardly will you find a delicious American recipe that has no meaty flavor especially when you move down south of the country. To add more nutrients, you may want your recipes to have some beans and even fruits to make the recipes nutrient-dense. Some of the things you can expect from this chapter are;

▪ Lean meat recipes that will lower your cholesterol while providing sufficient protein.

▪ Poultry meat recipes that will nourish your body with Iron, B-vitamins and other essential minerals and Phyto-nutrients, and

▪Crowd-pleasing meaty recipes you can mix with other varieties of ingredients.

Recipe #5: The Smokey Pot With Boston Beans

This American baked bean-stew will transform your day, with its special pork loin steaks alongside shredded Ham hock.

Preparation time: 40 minutes
Servings: 4

Ingredients:

- 2 tablespoons of olive oil,
- 2 crushed garlic cloves,
- 2 tablespoons of paprika (smoked),
- 500g of quartered pork loins,
- 2 cans of Cannellini beans (rinsed and drained),
- 400g of Passata,
- 2 tablespoons of Chipotle paste,
- 1 tablespoon of brown sugar (dark and soft),
- 100g of Ham hocks (shredded into large pieces),
- 4-5 slices of crusty wheat bread,
- 1 handful of parsley leaves (chopped roughly).

Direction

1. Heat the oven to about 180 °C, then mix the oil with the paprika, garlic before rubbing the mix on the pork.

2. Get a large shallow ovenproof dish and inside, mix the Cannellini beans with the Chipotle, Passata, ham hock and brown sugar. Make sure you immerse the pork into the beans, before baking in the oven for about 40 minutes until the pork has been cooked through.

3. Toast the bread and serve it on one side before sprinkling the parsley over the pork and beans. Serve immediately.

Recipe #6: The Griddled Chicken Served With Corn Cobs And Gem Lettuce Salad.

Americans love sweet corn, served with paprika and spiced chicken. The salad will even make the recipe more delicious and healthier.

Preparation time: 35 minutes
Servings: 4

Ingredients:

- 4 small chicken breasts (skinless),
- 2 garlic cloves (crushed),
- 1 tablespoon of paprika,
- 1 lemon (juice),
- 2 tablespoons of olive oil,
- 2 corn cobs,
- 4 Gem Lettuce (Quartered lengthwise),
- ½ long cucumber (diced)
- ½ teaspoon of red pepper(optional),
- ½ teaspoon of salt(optional).

Direction

1. Cut the chicken into halves (lengthwise), which means you will have 8 chicken strips. Get a bowl and inside, mix the paprika with the lemon juice, and garlic. Add 1 tablespoon of olive oil and add some

seasonings such as pepper and salt (optional). Toss the chicken with the mix and allow them to sit for about 15 minutes before you proceed.

2. Get a griddle pan and heat it before brushing it with the remaining 1 tablespoon of oil. Cook the chicken on each side for about 4-5 minutes until they start turning golden brown, Brush the chicken with any oil left before you griddle the corn cobs (turn them to ensure they cook evenly)- you can continue cooking until the corns have been lightly charred. Once cooked, remove the corns and cut off the kernels.

3. Get a new bowl and inside, mix your lettuce with the cucumber and then top up with the corn and chicken. You can also drizzle on top, your favorite dressing.

Recipe #7: The Crispy Cashew Chicken

Crispy cashew taste with chicken is one amazing taste you want to try out this summer.

Servings: 5-10
Total preparation time: 30 minutes

Ingredients:

- Two egg whites,
- 1 ¼ cups of cashew nuts (finely chopped)
- 2 chicken breasts (skinned, boned and thinly sliced)
- 2 cups of peanut (you may use vegetable oil)
- 1 quarter cup of cornstarch
- 1 teaspoon of brown sugar,
- 2 teaspoons of salt,
- 1 teaspoon of dry sherry

Direction:

1. Get a little bowl and inside, mix the salt, with starch, the sugar, and the sherry, and then make use of a separate bowl where you beat the egg white, after this, you can add your cornstarch mixture, in the second bowl before stirring gently until they blend perfectly.
2. Put the cashew inside a new and clean plate and your chicken slices one after the other into the egg mixture and make sure the chicken has been coated perfectly.

3. You can now add your peanut oil inside the Wok, and with the aid of tempura, make sure the rack hooks are positioned in the proper way.

4. Get your oil into a pan and heat it over moderate heat to about 380 degrees and then put some 5-6 chickens inside at a time. Make sure you fry the chicken until they have changed color to golden brown, remove the chicken after frying them for about 5 minutes and rain them with the aid of the Tempura.

#8: Beef With The Lentil Burger

This is a delicious and quick lunch for a busy day.

Servings: 4

Preparation time: 35 minutes

Ingredients

- 1 Can of rinsed and drained lentils,
- 250-320g of lean beef mince,
- 1 small coarsely grated zucchini,
- 1 large egg,
- 1 can of halved cherry tomatoes,
- 2 tablespoons of coriander,
- 2 tablespoons of olive oil spray,
- 1/3 of a cup of non-fat hummus,
- 4 splits and toasted wholegrain rolls,
- 1 trimmed and thinly sliced Lebanese cucumber, and
- 2 cups of baby spinach leaves.

Direction

1. Mix the lentils with the zucchini, egg, and mince, in a large bowl before seasoning with optional salt and pepper. Shape the mix into 4 different patties, and place them on a baking tray. Cover and place the patties in the refrigerator for about 10 minutes.
2. In a separate bowl, combine the coriander with the tomato while the patties are chilling in the fridge.

3. Spray your barbecue grill with the spray oil, and heat it over medium heat. Cook the patties on each side for about 4 minutes, until they are slightly charred and cooked. Spray the hummus on top of the base of the rolls, and then top with the spinach, Cucumber, tomato, and patties as well as the remaining roll.

Chapter 3: Scrumptious And Filling Snacks Recipes

In this section, you will learn some of the best American snacks you can indulge in, without adding too many calories, in between the full course meals. These are very filling snacks that you can get stuck unto, and these include;

- Pies,
- Hot chocolate crackers or biscuits, and
- Brownies

Recipe #9: The Choc-Chip Pecan Pie

This is a mix of chocolate with pecan treat that can get everyone filled up all day. It is one of the best American snack options you should consider right now!

Preparation time: 1 hour 25 minutes
Servings: 10-12

Ingredients:

- 5 cups of plain flour,
- 4 tablespoons of cubed salted vegetable butter,
- 1 tablespoon of icing sugar,
- 2 cups of cream cheese.

For the Icing, you need the following ingredients

- 5 tablespoons of salted vegetable butter,
- ½ a cup of maple syrup,
- 3-4 tablespoons of light brown sugar,
- 4 large beaten eggs,
- 1 teaspoon of vanilla extract,
- 2 cups of finely chopped pecans,
- 1 large bar of dark chocolate (chopped).

Direction

1. Prepare the pastry first. Add the ingredients inside the food processor blend until the mix looks like breadcrumbs, then drizzle up to 3 tablespoons of

cold water through a funnel while the processor's blade is still running. Tip the mix on a work surface and knead them briefly into medium-size balls. Pat the balls into a disc and let it chill for about 20 minutes in the fridge before you pre-heat the oven at 200 °C.

2. Remove your pastry from the fridge and then allow it to stay at room temperature for about 5 minutes. Add flour to your work surface before unwrapping the pastry and then roll them into circles with a 1 British pound coin. Use the pastry to line a 23cm round fluted tin, then press your pastry very well into the corners as well as the sides (make sure you leave no gaps). Line it with baking parchment before you fill it with baking beans. Bake in the oven for about 20 minutes, until the sides become set before removing the parchment and the beans. Return the pastry to the oven and bake further for 5 minutes until it turns golden brown. Trim down your pastry to make it at par with the top of the fluted tin.

3. While baking, weigh the butter and syrup into a pan and add ¼ teaspoon of salt. Heat the butter until it melts and stirs until it becomes smooth. Remove the mix from heat and cool for about 10 minutes. Reduce the temperature of the oven to 160°C.

4. Get a bowl and inside, beat the eggs, add the syrup mix alongside the pecans and vanilla and mix until

properly combined. Pour half of the mix inside a tart case before you scatter it on top of half of the chocolate chips (or crushed chocolate bar). Bake inside the middle shelf of the oven for about 55 minutes until it becomes set. Remove them from the oven and allow it to cool for about 2 hours before you serve.

Recipe #10: The Bourbon With Black Cherry And Bacon Brownies

This is American tray-bake brownies that comprise of everything you love- chocolate, and bacon.

Preparation time: 55 minutes
Servings: 12 pieces

Ingredients:

- 2-3 cups of dried and sour cherries,
- ½ a cup of bourbon,
- 1 teaspoon of Cinnamon,
- ¼ of a cup of maple syrup,
- 6 rashers of smoked and streaky bacon,
- 2 teaspoons of brownie mix, and
- 2 teaspoons of cocoa powder (for dusting).

Direction

1. Heat the oven to about 180 °C. Get a small pan, and inside, warm the cherries inside the bourbon. And let it infuse for about 20 minutes.
2. Meanwhile, get a get a pan and inside mix the Cinnamon with the maple syrup and then brush both sides of your bacon with the mix. Lay your rashers over the rack, and before you set it on top of a roasting tin covered inside a foil and roast. Roast the mix and occasionally basting it inside the

syrup (this should take roughly 20 minutes until they turn brown). Allow them to cool on the rack while you prepare the brownie mix.

3. Prepare the brownie mix according to the recipe direction, then heat the oven to the appropriate temperature before you drain the bourbon-covered cherries- add these to the brownie mix. Chop the bacon into pieces before adding them to the mix. Bake for about 15-20 minutes and then cool completely for about 5 minutes while dusting with cocoa powder. Slice them into squares before serving.

Recipe #11: Fresh Fruit With Yoghurt Ice Pops

One of the perfect treats for the kids, they will surely thank you for this.

Preparation time: 4 minutes
Cooking time: 42 minutes
Servings: 8

Ingredients:

• 2 cups of a mix of strawberries, raspberries, blueberries, and diced bananas,

• 2 cups of vanilla or plain yogurt,

• ¼ cup of brown sugar,

• 8 popsicle sticks, and

• 8 small paper cups.

Direction:

1. Place all the fruits and the yogurt in a blender, then cover and blend until the mix becomes smooth or chunky, as desired. (4 minutes)

2. Fill up the paper cups 3/4 full with the fruit mix, and cover each with a strip of aluminum foil. (2 minutes)

3. Pop in a Popsicle stick at the center of the aluminum foil. You can freeze the cups and their contents for about 40 minutes and remove the aluminum foils when serving. (41 minutes).

Recipe #12: Simple And Fast Vanilla Cupcakes

Amazing American cupcakes for those who cherish the tasty and stomach-friendly cupcakes.

Preparation time: 7minutes
Cooking time: 21
Servings: 12

Ingredients:

- 6 ounces of cake flour,
- 5 ounces of brown sugar,
- 6 ounces of softened unsalted butter,
- 3 large slightly beaten eggs,
- ½ teaspoon of vanilla essence,
- 1 teaspoon of baking powder

For the icing, add some sifted sugar (optional).

Direction:

1. Pre-heat the oven to 350-degrees F and prepare some 12 paper cupcakes in some muffin tins. (2 minutes)
2. Mix the butter and sugar in a bowl, and cream with an electric mixer for about 2 minutes, until the mix becomes creamy. (2 minutes)

3. Add the beaten eggs, and mix, add the vanilla, and then sift in your flour and baking powder and mix further for about a minute. (1 minute)

4. Spoon the batter into the cupcake cases, and fill them at about 2/3 full then place in the middle of the oven rack. (2 minutes)

5. Bake for about 20 minutes and remove, and let it cool for few minutes and serve immediately. (21 minutes).

Chapter 4: Amazing Seafood And Poultry Recipes

Seafood has become part of traditional American delicacies because of the numerous benefits they offer, aside from the fact that they taste so wonderfully delicious. Some of the things to expect from this chapter are;

• Seafood recipes that are lower in fat and cholesterol for a healthier heart,

•Seafood recipes that are high in Omega 3 fatty acids that are friendly to your body system.

• seafood that is well crafted and blended with different vegetables to enhance their health benefits.

Recipe #13: Baked Fish Served With Vegetables

Total prep: 35 minutes

Servings: 4

Ingredients

- 2 pieces of Zucchinis cut into wedges,
- 2 pieces of red onions cut into wedges,
- 3 pieces of large tomatoes cut into wedges,
- A quarter cup of pitted black olives,
- A quarter cup of olive oil,
- 4 thick skinless fish fillets,
- 1 tablespoon of lemon juice,
- tablespoon of Dijon mustard, and
- ½ a cup of chopped parsley leaf.

Direction

1. Pre-heat the oven to about 200-degree C.
2. Toss the mix of zucchini, tomato, onion, olives and a tablespoon of oil in a baking dish, and then brush the top and side of the fish with a tablespoon of oil before placing the fish on vegetables. Place the fishes inside the oven and then bake for about 30 minutes until they are cooked through.

3. In another bowl, simply whisk together, the lemon juice, garlic, mustard and remaining oil, to make the dressing.
4. Split the cooked vegetables between the plates, and top each plate with a piece of fish.
5. Drizzle the dressings on each fish and divide the parsley on them also.

Serve immediately.

Recipe #14: Ginger Sesame Salmon

Preparation time: 25

Servings: 1-2

Ingredients:

- 4 ounces of Salmon,
- ¼ cup of soy sauce,
- 2 tablespoons of Balsamic vinegar,
- ½ teaspoon of sesame oil,
- 2-inch chunk of peeled, grated ginger,
- A teaspoon of olive oil,
- A teaspoon of sesame seeds, and
- A teaspoon of minced green onion.

Direction:

1. Marinate the Salmon for about 15 minutes in the soy sauce mixed with balsamic vinegar, sesame oil, and ginger. Get a hot non-stick skillet, and coat it with the olive oil. Remove the Salmon from the marinade and then sauté the fish until it becomes firm (make sure the fish is sautéed on both sides).
2. Sprinkle the salmon inside the pan, and alongside the sesame seeds. Remove the salmon from the pan and then garnish with minced green onion. Serve immediately.

Recipe #15: The Hearty Fish Stew

Total prep: 35 minutes

Servings: 4

Ingredients

- A tablespoon of extra light olive oil,
- 4, finely chopped garlic cloves,
- 1 teaspoon of ground turmeric,
- 2 cans of whole peeled tomatoes,
- 1 can of rinsed and drained cannellini beans,
- 2 lean fillets, cut into large pieces,
- 1/3 of a cup of chopped fresh coriander leaves,
- 3-4 crusty whole grain loaves of bread.

Direction

1. Heat the olive oil inside a large saucepan, and over medium heat. Add the garlic and stir for about 60 seconds. Add the turmeric and cook further for about 30 seconds, then stir in the tomatoes plus a cup of water before covering. Bring to boil immediately, for about 10 minutes and thereafter, let it simmer.
2. Add the beans and then return it to boil, cover and add the fish and allow the mix to cook for about 5 minutes.

3. Spoon the stews into different bowls, and sprinkle your coriander leaves before serving with bread rolls.

Recipe #16: The Lemon Salmon Served With Kaffir Lime

The strong taste of lemon in this recipe makes the recipe more welcoming for those who can handle the dish.

Total prep: 40 minutes
Servings: 8

Ingredients:
- A whole side of salmon fillet,
- A thinly sliced lemon,
- 2 kaffir torn lime leaves,
- A quartered and bruised lemongrass stalk,
- A cup of loosely packed coriander leaves,
- A cup of fresh coriander leaves.

Direction:
1. Pre-heat the oven to about 170 C, and then place some foil sheets and make them slightly overlapping on a baking dish. Place some Salmon on the foil and then top the fish with lemon and lime leaves plus the lemongrass and coriander. You may season with a half tablespoon of salt and pepper.
2. Bring the long side of the foil to the center before folding the seal. Roll the ends in order to close up the salmon and then bake for about 30 minutes before cooling to room temperature. Transfer the

mix to a platter and top up with some coriander before serving.

Chapter 5: Low-Calorie Bread And Related Recipes

Bread goes with virtually many other recipes and is fast becoming part of group eat-outs in the United States today. This chapter offer recipes with the following features;

• Low-calorie ketogenic bread, that will not trigger a sharp increase in blood sugar.

• Gluten-free bread recipes for those suffering from gluten-allergy, and

Recipe #17: The Keto Banana Loaf

Preparation time: 1 hour

Servings: 3

Ingredients:
- 12 ounces of soft cream cheese,
- 5 large eggs,
- A cup of mashed bananas,
- ½ cup of soy protein powder,
- A teaspoon of baking powder,
- A teaspoon of baking powder,
- 4 teaspoons of Splenda (sugar substitute),
- 2 teaspoons of grated lemon peel,
- A cup of unprocessed wheat bran, and
- A cup of whole almond meal.

Direction:

1. Pre-heat the oven to about 325-degrees F, and then butter lightly, the mini loaf pans. Cut some strips of waxed paper to fit the bottoms of the pan, and allow them to hang over the edges.
2. Get the cream cheese and eggs in the electric mixer bowl, and beat until flat. Add the remaining eggs (one at a time), add all other ingredients and then beat at a slow speed. Add the nuts and bran and spoon the batter into the pans. Bake the bread for about an hour until done and serve immediately.

Recipe #18: The Gluten-Free Coconut And Almond Bread

Preparation time: 1 hour
Servings: 2-20 slices (1 loaf)

Ingredients:

- One, 3/4 of almond flour,
- 1 ½ tablespoons of coconut flour,
- ¼ of a cup of ground flaxseed,
- ¼ tablespoon of salt,
- 1 teaspoon of baking soda,
- 4-5 large eggs,
- ¼ of a cup of coconut oil,
- 1 teaspoon of a natural sweetener such as stevia,
- 1 tablespoon of apple cider vinegar.

Direction

1. Pre-heat the oven to about 350-degrees F, and then grease the loaf of the pan. Mix the almond, and coconut flour, alongside the flaxseed, salt, and baking soda, inside a food processor. Pulse the ingredients together, before you add the eggs, vinegar, and oil.
2. Pour the mix or batter into the loaf pan, and bake for about 30 minutes at the 350-degree F in the

oven. Let the bread cool for few minutes before serving.

Recipe #19: The American Cornbread

You may want to prepare this recipe ahead of time, and then warm it for a few minutes later when you need them.

Preparation time: 55 minutes
Servings: 8-10 slices

Ingredients:

- 50g of slightly salted butter(melted),
- 250g of fine cornmeal or polenta (a little extra for dusting),
- 320g can of drained sweet corn,
- ½ a cup of buttermilk,
- 4 medium to large eggs,
- 1 tablespoon of brown sugar,
- 2 cups of plain flour,
- 2 teaspoons of baking powder, and
- 1 teaspoon of Bicarbonate of soda.

Direction

1. Heat the oven to about 190 degrees Celsius, and get a 900g loaf tin (brush this with butter), dust the tin with polenta, and tip half of the sweet corn into your food processor, alongside the remaining ingredients plus ½ a teaspoon of salt. Blend the mixture until it becomes smooth, and then remove

the blade before stirring through the remaining sweet corn.

2. Pour the batter from the food processor into the tin and scatter on top the last sweet corn before baking in the oven for about 50 minutes until it has turned golden and risen. Push a skewer through the center and when you remove it, it should come out with some moist crumbs. You may return the batter into the oven and make for between 5-10 extra minutes until properly done.

Cool off the loaf inside its tin for about 10 minutes before transferring it unto a wire rack. You store it in the refrigerator if you are not serving it immediately.

Chapter 6: Amazing Soups And Stews Worth Relishing

Soups and stews have always been part of American dishes for centuries, they are unique in every way and there seems to be no food they are not compatible with. Some of the information you will learn from this chapter are;

•Special seasonal recipes that can help you prevent flu and other seasonal infections,

• Soups with high concentrations of antioxidants that can reduce your risks of cancer and boost your immunity, significantly.

Recipe #20: The Tomato Soup

This is one of the perfect soups you should consume in the winter season to reduce your risks of flu and some other viral infections.

Cooking time: 30 minutes
Servings: 1-2

Ingredients

- 1kg of ripe tomatoes,
- 1 Medium chopped onion,
- 2 cloves of garlic,
- A large carrot,
- 2 celery sticks,
- 2 tablespoons of olive oil,
- 2 teaspoon of tomato puree,
- 2 bay leaves,
- 1 liter of hot vegetable stock, and
- Some fresh basil for garnishing.

Direction

1. Prepare your veggies by washing the tomatoes and slicing into halves, peel the onion, carrot, and garlic and cut into pieces. Chop your celery into smaller sizes too. Add your olive oil unto a pan, and heat over a low heat before adding your onion, garlic, carrot, and celery.

2. Cook for about 10 minutes for the veggies to get soft. Add the puree, tomatoes and black pepper, then add the bay leaves before allowing the mix to simmer over low heat for about 10 minutes. Stir in the veggies and then the hot stock and cook gently for about 15 minutes over low heat.

3. Stir soup every 5 minutes to distribute evenly, then turn the heat off when cooked and remove bay leaves. Pour the mix into a blender and blend smoothly. Serve immediately with basil leaves.

Recipe #21: The Minestrone Soup

Packed with anti-oxidant foods that boosts immunity and reduce risks of certain infections.

Preparation time: It takes about 50 minutes to prepare.

Servings: 5

Ingredients:

- 1 tablespoon of cold-pressed rapeseed oil,
- 1 finely chopped medium or large onion,
- 2 big crushed clove garlic,
- 2 stalks of chopped celery,
- 2 medium chopped zucchini courgettes,
- 8 medium chopped carrots,
- 100g of chopped Spinach,
- three 400g tins of chopped tomatoes,
- 150g of strand pasta,
- 5 pints of vegetable stock,
- 2 tablespoon of tomato puree,
- ½ teaspoon freshly ground pepper with salt, and
- 1 handful of freshly chopped parsley.

Direction:

1. Prepare the soup be sautéing the onion in garlic, inside the rapeseed oil until it becomes soft and translucent, add the celery and the courgettes

alongside the carrots and then cook for few minutes. Add your tomatoes, tomato puree, spinach, and vegetable stock, then mix very well before boiling. Reduce the heat and cover the mix gently to allow it simmer for about 15 minutes.

2. Add your pasta and then cook for extra 15 minutes, before seasoning (you can add fresh herbs if you want). Serve this soup immediately.

Recipe #22: The Poblano Black Bean Corn Soup

A delicious soup that goes with any other type of food

Cooking time: 12 minutes

Servings: 1-2

Ingredients:

- ¼ small, white diced onion,
- De-seeded ½ Poblano pepper,
- 2 cloves of minced garlic,
- ¼ teaspoon each of cumin powder and dried oregano,
- ½ teaspoon of olive oil,
- ½ of 15 ounces can of drained black beans,
- ½ cup of frozen and fresh corn,
- A teaspoon of Balsamic vinegar,
- A tablespoon of aged and well-grated parmesan cheese
- A cup of chicken stock

Direction

1. Sautee the onion with the Poblano pepper, minced garlic, cumin powder and oregano powder, inside the olive oil, for about 2 minutes over medium to high heat. Add the black beans, corn, balsamic vinegar, and chicken stock and let it simmer for

about 8 minutes, then add the parmesan cheese and serve hot.

Recipe #23: The Quick And Easy Vegetable Curry

Curry goes with bread and many other delicacies; this recipe is worth trying out.

Preparation time: 30 minutes
Servings: 5

Ingredients:
- 1 chopped onion
- a tablespoon of olive oil,
- 2 crushed garlic cloves,
- 2 tablespoons of curry powder,
- 2 tablespoons of tomato paste,
- 14.5 ounces (1 can) of diced tomatoes,
- 1 cube of vegetable bouillon,
- 1 ½ cups of water,
- ½ teaspoons of salt and pepper to taste, and
- 2 tablespoons of chopped fresh cilantro.

Direction:
1. Heat the oil and then sauté the onion and garlic inside a saucepan, over a medium heat, until they become golden, then stir inside the curry powder

and tomato paste and cook further for about 3 minutes.

2. Stir in the tomatoes, the vegetable bouillon cube, vegetables, water, salt and pepper and cook for 24 minutes until the vegetable becomes crunchy. Sprinkle the meal with fresh cilantro before serving.

Conclusion

Most people around the world believe that the typical American diet is filled with lots of sugar, salt, and trans-fatty components, whereas this is a misconception that the world needs to do away with. Americans love to eat healthily, and that means they love to cut back on the sugar, salt, high carbs and fatty foods that increase waist-line significantly within a short period of time, and this is the reason why this book has been written and well-researched to give all readers an insight into how American diets have evolved over time.

If you really want to enjoy the tasty American dishes that you can serve with your friends and family at different seasons of the year, then the **AMERICAN COOKBOOK** should be your guide. This book also gives you the room to become creative, especially when substituting one ingredient with another, depending on your preference.